Your Environment

Animal RIGHTS

Julia Allen

Margaret Iggulden

Franklin Watts
London • Sydney

How to use this book

This series has been developed for group use in the classroom, as well as for students reading on their own. Its differentiated text allows students of mixed reading abilities to enjoy reading and talking about the same topic.

① The main text and ② picture captions give essential information in short, simple sentences. They are set in the © Sassoon font as recommended by the National Literacy Strategy document *Writing in the Early Years*. This font style helps students bridge the gap between their reading and writing skills.

③ Below each picture caption is a subtext that explains the pictures in greater detail, using more complicated sentence structures and vocabulary.

④ Text backgrounds are cream or a soft yellow to reduce the text/background contrast to support students with visual processing difficulties or other special needs.

Introduction

Organisations all over the world are working to protect the rights of animals. ①

⬆ We can help others to treat animals with kindness. ②

③

Animals have been part of our lives for thousands of years. ④

PAPERBACK EDITION PRINTED 2008
© Aladdin Books Ltd 2005

Designed and produced by
Aladdin Books Ltd
2&3 Fitzroy Mews
London W1T 6DF

First published in 2005 by
Franklin Watts
338 Euston Road
London NW1 3BH

Franklin Watts Australia
Level 17/207 Kent Street
Sydney NSW 2000

Franklin Watts is a division of Hachette Children's Books

ISBN 978 0 7496 8166 1

Educational Consultant: J Holderness

Animal Rights Consultant: Freeman Wicklund, Humane Educator for Teachkind.org

Design: Ken Vail Graphic Design, Cambridge, UK

Picture Research: Gemma Cooper

A catalogue record for this book is available from the British Library.

Dewey Classification: 179'.3

Printed in Malaysia

CONTENTS

Introduction

For thousands of years, people have killed animals for food, clothing and sport.

Now, many people ask whether this should stop.

Organisations all over the world are working to protect the rights of animals. Pet owners, zookeepers, farmers and scientists are now more aware of animals' needs and rights than they used to be.

▷ **Do animals have the same rights as you?**

Like you, animals need food, water and a home, as well as the space and freedom to exercise. Most people believe that animals should not be hurt or frightened and that they should be treated with respect.

People say that animal rights are about protecting animals from cruelty.

Many work to stop the unnecessary suffering of animals. Others say human needs are more important. Do you agree?

Can animals suffer?

Most people believe they do suffer if they are injured or scared. Many of us have seen a cat or a dog hurt. Many people believe all animals, even hamsters and guinea pigs, have feelings too.

We can help others to treat animals with kindness.

Animal rights is about being kind and helping animals that cannot protect themselves from human beings. Animals have been part of our lives for thousands of years, either as pets, or on farms. We eat some animals and see exotic animals for entertainment in circuses and zoos. This book explains what animal rights are and what is happening to animals around the world. It also gives information about helping to look after animals.

Your pet's rights

How do you know if your pet is hungry, thirsty, happy or sad? How do you look after it? Pets need fresh food, clean water and a place that is theirs. Their bedding needs to be changed often.

In the past people thought that animals had no feelings at all. We now understand and accept that pets have rights.

◁ 'A dog is for life, not just for Christmas.'

This slogan reminds us that owning a dog is a long-term commitment. Sometimes people are given a dog at Christmas. After a few days, the excitement of having a new pet wears off. When no one wants to take the dog for a walk, it may be abandoned.

Pets are fun, but they need care, time and effort.

Pets also cost a lot of money to feed and look after. If your pet is ill you must take it to the vet – this can be expensive. Pets are part of the family. If a family is out all day, the choice of pet will be very important. Dogs, for example, need regular exercise and can get lonely if left for too long.

Pets need to eat a healthy diet.

Suzie is nine years old. She was given so many treats that she became overweight. This in turn created heart problems. Her owner was too ill to look after her. On arrival at the adoption centre, she was put on a diet and now she is healthier. Suzie was lucky and found a new home, but millions of pets will not. There are too many unwanted pets and not enough good homes.

Every day, cats and dogs are starved, abused and abandoned.

Most people, of course, believe that it is wrong for animals to be mistreated. They believe that pets and other animals have the right not to be injured or killed.

The use of animals

Experts tell us that humans originated in Africa. They then moved across the continents of the world.

At that time, they hunted and gathered food.

About 10,000 years ago, humans started farming. Later they learned to keep animals. We have lived closely with animals ever since.

⬆ **Tibetans in the Himalayas use yaks.**

For about two thousand years, Tibetan nomads have used yaks. These animals provide them with meat, wool, milk and cheese and so are highly prized. Yaks can also carry up to 150 kg over steep mountains.

The llama was used by the Incas.

The ancient Incas of South America treated the llama well. The animals gave them food and clothing, and could carry heavy burdens up and across the mountains. Llamas are still important in South America. They are even used in some areas to carry goods to people living in remote places.

Dogs have been part of our lives for thousands of years.

Over centuries, wild dogs gradually were tamed. Farmers still use dogs to shepherd animals around. They are very skillful at herding sheep and other animals.

Horses, mules and oxen are still used on some farms.

They may be used to plough the soil, and to do other farming work. However, in many parts of the world, tractors and other farm machines have replaced these animals.

Exotic animals

It has become fashionable for some people to keep exotic animals as pets.

These are caught in the wild and then sold in pet shops or over the internet.

Capturing, shipping and selling exotic animals reduces their numbers in the wild. Many have become endangered.

◁ **Some endangered animals are kept in people's homes.**

Tigers should live free in the forests of Asia, but in October 2003, a large Bengal tiger was rescued from a flat in New York. There are fewer than 6,000 tigers left in the wild, but there may be even more kept as pets in the US.

◪ There are laws against buying and selling wild animals.

Many countries have joined together in an agreement called the Convention on International Trade in Endangered Species (CITES) to protect wildlife all over the world. They started a police service that is trying to stop illegal trade in animals.

⬆ Exotic animals are bought as pets, but they have specific needs.

Some people like to keep tortoises. Exotic animals like these are often bought and kept without being fed properly. Tortoises need to eat a varied diet – if not, their shells weaken and they die. This may not be deliberate, but it is still cruelty.

⬇ Some animals are used for traditional medicine.

Eighty per cent of the population of the world use traditional medicine. Some of this comes from plants. However, in many traditional products, various parts of animals are used. Tigers, rhinos and leopards in particular are hunted for this trade. Already endangered, their numbers are declining rapidly.

Animals used for entertainment

Animals have been used for fun and entertainment since ancient times.

The ancient Romans enjoyed watching lions attacking people for sport. They had arenas throughout their empire.

Another favourite Roman pastime was chariot racing. Horse-drawn chariots were raced around the arena to see whose was the fastest.

▷ **People from various cultures have different views about animals and entertainment.**

Bullfighting has been a traditional pastime in Spain, Portugal, the South of France and South America for hundreds of years. However, people's opinions are changing. Over half the population of Spain is now against bullfighting. Many young people think these events are simply for old people. More and more places are banning bullfights.

There are laws to protect animals that are used in films.

Keiko, the Orca whale, was captured near Iceland in 1979 when he was two years old. Later he starred in the 'Free Willy' films. Film sets are inspected to check all the animals have clean and safe housing, and to make sure the stunts won't hurt or frighten the animals.

Orang-utans are being captured and used to entertain people.

In December 2004, orang-utans were found in some zoos in South-east Asia. They were dressed as boxers and encouraged to fight

each other. They were probably captured from the wild. Often, poachers kill the adults and steal the baby apes because they are easier to handle.

Using bears for entertainment is against the law in many places.

Many bears are taken from their forest homes. Every year, about one hundred bears are captured, leaving fewer bears in the wild. A bear sanctuary has been set up to help the bears that have been rescued.

Circuses

In the past, circuses were popular. No one thought it wrong to see animals performing. However, in the last twenty years, people's attitudes have changed. They feel it is degrading to make the animals perform tricks.

Now there are circuses that only have people performing. Millions of people around the world have been to see these circus shows.

◁ **Some circus animals may have little space to move around.**

They bob their heads and sway their bodies. This shows the animals are bored and distressed. The owners of a circus may be prosecuted for not looking after and protecting their animals.

⬅ This chimpanzee was a baby when he was captured in Africa. He was sold to a circus in South America.

He lived alone in a tiny wooden box for twenty years. He was rescued and taken back to Africa to a new home in Zambia. Now he is with other chimpanzees in their natural habitat.

⬆ Should modern circuses keep animals like this tiger?

Circuses may feature large wild animals, such as lions, tigers, elephants, giraffes and rhinos.

Because circuses have to travel long distances, some people believe it is difficult for them to look after the animals properly.

⬇ Circus animals need proper care.

Horses enjoy grazing in fields. They need plenty of space for proper exercise. Not all circus horses are well looked after. They may be kept in cramped conditions, or may be poorly fed. If a horse is unwell, not all circuses will contact a vet.

Hunting animals

In the late 19th and early 20th century, rich people went to India and Africa and hunted big game. They came back with trophies – leopard skins, elephant tusks and rhino horn.

However, in the last part of the 20th century, people realised that these animals were becoming scarce. People campaigned against hunting.

Now, many people feel that these awesome animals should be allowed the right to live and be free.

◁ **Some countries have protected areas for wild animals.**

Tourists can go on safari to watch wild animals in their natural habitat. Tourism can bring a lot of money into a country. Many governments now see the benefit of protecting these wild animals. They are working harder to fight illegal hunting.

⬅ Endangered species are being hunted again in some African countries.

In the last few years, companies have been set up to organise hunts for wild animals. They want to attract hunters who will pay a lot of money to come to Africa to shoot these animals.

⬇ Wolves are hunted in some of the states in the USA.

Wolves are protected in many states. However, against public opinion, in 2004 the government in Alaska passed a law stating that 900 wolves could be shot. Marksmen in planes shoot the wolves. They are easily seen against the snow so are easy to kill.

⬆ Big cats are some of the animals which are being hunted.

Lions, elephants and hippos are being killed in huge numbers. Some animals, such as gorillas and leopards, are hunted and sold as 'bushmeat'. Cheetahs are killed for their beautiful fur. This is used to make expensive clothes.

Zoos: prisons or education?

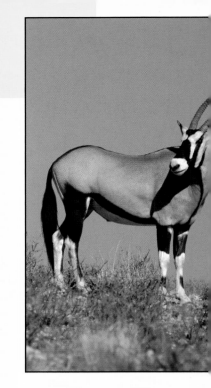

Do we have the right to take animals from the wild and keep them in captivity?

There are about 750 zoos all over the world. Many people come to see the animals for entertainment.

It is argued that these zoos help to educate people. Otherwise they would not be aware of these animals. In the zoos they can learn about them.

▷ **However, not all zoos keep their animals in good conditions.**

Some animals are kept in cages with no room to exercise. They walk up and down in a small space for hours every day, whereas in the wild they can roam over miles and miles.

⬅ Are zoos successful at re-introducing animals back into the wild?

In the 1960s, the Oryx was still hunted in Arabia. By the 1970s few were left, so they were bred in captivity. Eventually 400 were returned to the wild, but many died on the journey. By 1999, only 100 were left.

⬆ Animals like giraffes can roam freely in National Parks.

Many people believe that we should let animals live freely in their own habitat. Silver-backed gorillas live in Central Africa. The local people have hunted them, but now there are large areas where they are safe and free.

⬇ Zoos are breeding lemurs successfully in captivity.

Zoos are helping to breed and therefore conserve rare animals. There are some zoos where the animals are the most important factor. There is a huge amount of space for the animals and some, like these lemurs from Madagascar, are hard for visitors to spot.

Animals used for clothing

Thousands of years ago humans wore animal skins to keep warm. They hunted animals for food and did not waste anything. They always respected the spirit of each animal they killed.

Native American Indians and other peoples around the world still have a great respect for animals. They do not understand why other people haven't.

◁ **Many people do not agree with people wearing fur and leather.**

Twenty years ago in the USA and UK there was an anti-fur campaign. Campaigners for animal rights changed public opinion about wearing fur. As a result, it was considered unacceptable. Many shops that sold fur closed down.

⬆ One fur coat = about 40 minks or foxes (above).

Some of these animals may have been caught in a trap. The animals suffer. They may stay there for hours or days trying to escape, often in great pain. Other kinds of animals are caught in these traps, too. Many people feel that these traps are cruel and inhumane.

⬅ In 2004, some famous film and pop stars wore boots made of rabbit fur.

They became a fashion item and thousands of these boots were sold in high street shops all over the world. Some people decided to wear fake fur instead.

⬇ Chiru antelope are hunted in Tibet.

There used to be hundreds of thousands of them, but now there are only about 60,000. They are an endangered species because they are hunted for almost every part of their body. Their wool, the softest and warmest wool in the world, is smuggled into India. It is sold as Shah Toosh, 'The King of the Wool'. This is woven into shawls that are sold in Europe and North America.

Animals and food

All over the world people have different ideas about the foods they eat. For example, in France horsemeat is eaten. In some countries dog meat is eaten. What is the difference between eating a cow and eating a horse?

△ **Pork, sausage and bacon are all foods made from pigs.**

▷ **Chicken is a popular meat in many countries.**

In many countries, pigs are farmed intensively. Their whole life is spent in stalls so small that they cannot turn around. On other farms, pigs roam freely. The piglets can even stay with their mother and live a natural life.

Chicken has been farmed intensively for many years. People are now concerned about the way chickens are kept. Many have begun to buy organic or free range chickens. The meat is tastier, with less added water.

Some people think catching fish on hooks is cruel.

However, many people prefer to eat fish instead of meat. The demand for fish has increased hugely. Instead of catching fish on lines and hooks, farmers have begun to farm fish. For example, salmon are grown in huge vats next to the sea. They are fed, and when the salmon are large enough they are killed and sent to food outlets, such as supermarkets.

More farmers are changing to traditional farming methods.

People are now very concerned about the way farm animals are treated. They would prefer that animals live as natural a life as possible before being killed locally. More and more farmers, therefore, are changing to natural, traditional methods of farming.

Animal testing for research

Why are animals used for research? Scientists say that they must find cures for different diseases. But first they must test drugs on animals to see if they are safe for human beings.

Many millions of people have been helped by the drugs developed in this way. For example, those who suffered from epilepsy, like the artist van Gogh, would have had an easier life if modern drugs had been available in their lifetime.

▷ A new drug can take years to develop.

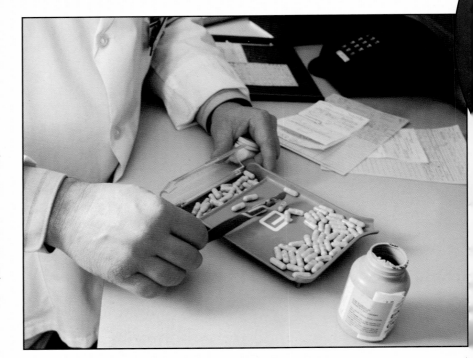

It can cost millions of pounds and take many years for a new medicine to be produced. Many people feel animal testing for medical research is worthwhile. Modern medicines have made many life-threatening illnesses a thing of the past. This is in part thanks to animal testing.

◁ Cosmetics are tested on animals.

Campaigners against animal testing ask if experimenting on animals is a good price to pay for developing new kinds of make-up. If you decide not to use products that have been tested on animals, then read the labels to make sure.

◁ Many products are tested on animals.

Animals are used to test a wide range of products. In addition to medicines and cosmetics, soap, shampoo, hairspray and laundry detergent are tested on animals.

▽ Some people ask why use animals in medical research at all.

Campaigners against animal testing say that animals are different species to human beings. They also say that in spite of the many experiments, a cure for cancer is yet to be found. In fact, plants in Madagascar have helped to cure different forms of leukaemia, especially in children. Perhaps more money should be put into plant research.

Do we need animal testing?

All over the world, scientists experiment on millions of rats and mice every day. However, animal rights campaigners believe that human beings are very different to these animals and so react differently to drugs than they do.

They suggest that there are now many other alternatives to animal testing.

With the development in computers, perhaps programmes using 'virtual humans' will take the place of live animals.

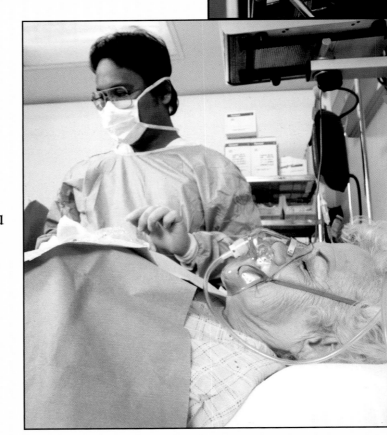

▷ **A drug may be safer for animals than for people.**

Some 'tested' drugs have been found to cause humans problems. For example, a drug that was meant to help people with heart problems was tested on animals. None of the animals tested developed any serious problems. It was thought the drug was safe. However, when taken by humans, some people suffered serious side-effects.

◁ People have volunteered to be tested rather than animals.

This has been found to be far more reliable than using animals. Computers can also be used instead of animal testing. The rapid development of technology means that experiments can be carried out on 'virtual human beings'.

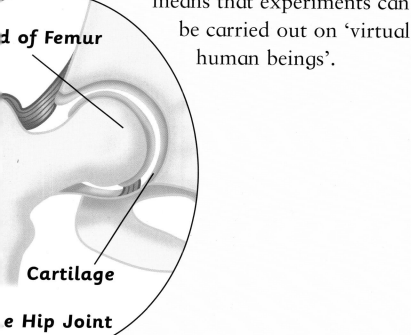

d of Femur

Cartilage

e Hip Joint

△ The inventor John Charnley did not use animal tests.

He was against such experiments. His invention for an artificial hip is still thought to be the best and is used by doctors today.

▽ Do we use too many chemicals in the 21st century?

Most people would prefer to have medicines available when they're ill. However, many products are very similar. Do we really need, or want, ten types of cough mixture or cold remedy to choose from? Before chemicals and drugs were invented people used natural ingredients to cure diseases. More and more doctors are now turning to natural remedies, rather than drugs.

Religion and animals

Native American Indians believe we must respect the spirit of all creatures.

When they hunted buffalo they only killed what they needed and then used its meat, skin and bones for food, clothing and shelter.

When Europeans came to the US, they hunted the buffalo to extinction. They killed far more than they needed.

▷ Some cultures believe that when we are born, we are given a particular animal to guide us in our lives.

This animal spirit has the same personal traits that we have. For example, if you are a confident person, perhaps your animal spirit is a peacock. Native American Indians believe that you can ask your animal spirit to help you.

Buddhism teaches people to respect nature and the environment.

Buddhists believe that animals have a right to life. Strict Buddhists are vegetarians and believe that animals and people should live peacefully together. Buddhist monks look after many animals, for example, Tibetan macaques. They are protected, fed and treated with respect, as all life is.

All religions teach that we should respect animals.

In the past, Judaism and Christianity taught that animals were put on the Earth for human beings. The Bible, however, never said that it was right to make animals suffer or to be cruel to them in any way. The Greek philosopher, Aristotle, did teach, however, that animals were on this planet for our use. This idea had a huge influence on Europeans.

Respect for all animals is taught in Hinduism and Islam.

Hindus believe that all animals should be treated as if they were your own son or daughter. They also believe the cow is a sacred animal. They treat cows with great respect and do not kill or eat them.

What can you do?

People often say that something is terrible or awful but that there is nothing that can be done about it.

This is not true. Something can be done. Things can be changed for the better.

Perhaps you have decided after reading this book that you want to help protect the rights of animals. You want them to be treated kindly, and with compassion.

▷ **Find out about animal rights and animal welfare.**

Ask your parents or teacher if you may search the internet or ask animal welfare organisations to send you information. They have packs for young people. Many people have strong feelings about animal rights. If you know more about the topic you will be able to make your own decisions.

◁ Ask your teacher if you may invite a speaker to your school.

You could contact the Blue Cross, the RSPCA, PETA or other animal charities. Ask them to come to your school to give a talk. They may have posters and leaflets you can put up in school about animal rights and animal welfare.

△ Look after your pet.

Make a note of when your pet gets its check-up with the vet. Help your parents with the care your pet needs. Walk the dog, brush the cat, feed the hamster. Your pet (and your parents) will appreciate it!

Glossary

Abuse – Mistreatment, injury or harm.

Captivity – When an animal is kept in a confined space, such as a cage.

CITES – Convention on International Trade in Endangered Species.

Compassion – A strong feeling of love and protection for people, animals and all living creatures.

Conservation – Work that is done to protect wildlife.

Extinction – When a species of animal or plant dies out completely, so that none are left alive.

Inhumane – When people treat animals cruelly.

Sanctuary – A place where animals are protected.

Species – A unique type of plant or animal such as the Bengal tiger.

Vegetarian – People who do not eat meat or fish, or animal products.

Welfare – Well-being, comfort and security.

INDEX

Photocredits

Abbreviations: l-left, r-right, b-bottom, t-top, c-centre, m-middle

30br - Brand X. Back cover tl, tr, 2mr, 3mr, 5ml, 5br, 6bl, 6-7t, 6-7mr, 7tr, 11ml, 25br, 30-31t, 31ml - Comstock. 16-17tm 16bl, 17ml, 19ml, 24br, 26br, 26-27t, 27br - Corbis. 1, 8l, 8tr, 9tr, 14tr, 19br, 24-25tm, 29br - Corel Stock Photos. Front cover tr, 3tr, 10bm, 10tr, 11br, 12br, 12-13t, 13bl, 13tr, 15br, 17br, 18-19t, 21tl, 28br - Digital Stock. Front cover c, b, 3tr 13bl, 16mr, 22ml, 23bl, 25ml - Digital Vision. 10-11tm, 20bl, 20br, 21br - Ingram Publishing. Front cover tl, 4-5t, 14bl, 15ml - John Foxx Images. 28-29t, 29ml - John Hollingsworth. 8-9b, 10ml, 18br, 22-23tm - Photodisc. 4br - Select Pictures. 27ml SGA Illustration & Design. 23br - Stockbyte.